You Are About to Do Great Things 2

JOE BULL

Kingdom Builders Publications LLC

© 2020 Joseph Bull
You Are About to do Great Things 2
Kingdom Builders Publications, LLC

All rights reserved. No part of this book may be reproduced or transmitted in any form or by any means without written permission from the author.

Printed in the USA

ISBN
978-0-578-76298-2
Soft Cover
Library of Congress Control Number
2020918036

Authored by
Joe Bull

Editor
Louise James
Kingdom Builders Publications

Cover Design
LoMar Designs
Picture for cover
Image | 109893899 dreamstime.com
Other graphics are free online pictures by BING

A SHAKENING IN THE WORLD

A dark cloud is passing over us.

What does this mean for time?

You called us when we think we're not good enough.

There were warnings but we ignored your voice.

Fear won't take over.

My trust is in you.

A shakening in the world is happening now.

How long will we go on listening to man?

The journey does not end now.

Look at what's going on in the world,

...and they didn't mention Jesus.

Joe Bull

ANY GIANT YOU FACE

Sometimes things don't go your way,

You did what you could,

Now let God step in.

Now He is able to take on things bigger than you,

His word is true.

Any Giant you face will have its day,

Be patient and let God use you.

The intimidation is to bring fear,

That Giant is your promotion.

Any Giant you face will have its day,

Be patient.

The flesh hurts, but God is our peace.

ASK FOR HELP

No matter how tough it gets, we have to move on.

I mean, we can't fight the battles by ourselves without asking for help from above.

Lord seems like I need you more and more

Negativity brushes threw my mind.

How can it be this way?

I know you'll strike it down,

It doesn't belong in my mind

I'm asking for help

I need you every day.

People are doing things their way.

Without you, people hurt others,

We need to ask for help.

AT THE PARK

I heard the sound of the rivers,
There were birds singing all around
Then I looked up to enjoy the blue skies and the sunshine as I sat there on the park bench.
At the park, I saw the swans and the ducks walking by the river.
Kids were playing with a smile
The grown folks were having a picnic, and they been out here for a while.
At the park, some people were playing tennis, getting exercise
You could smell the steaks and hotdogs somebody was grilling.
I looked across the street, at a house they was having a family cookout.
For some, the park was their getaway.
As I sat and enjoy the blue Skies and sunshine at the park.

DARKER NIGHTS

In these times the nights are darker,

A lost daughter who went back to the world,

They would preach at her, but she thought they were trying to stop her from living,

So she started hanging out in the dark nights with her friends,

In time she will see, the nights will only get darker out here

It's everyone for themselves,

So pray for her and the many out there, still in the dark nights,

The world offers pleasure but after its gone you're still alone.

There's someone else who also felt He was alone,

Jesus is the light for anyone who's in those darker nights, For those who tried everything out there,

In time, they will see the dark nights only become darker.

DON'T JUST GO BY WHAT YOU SEE

I'm in a place where I say, Lord I need you more,

I have to keep you close to me,

Sometimes when you move too fast,

You take your eyes off the prize,

Don't just go by what you see,

You're hoping it would be better,

Wait... It will.

Don't just go by what you see,

I have to keep You close to me,

In time, You will reveal why things don't happen when we want them to,

He's always around.

He's always working.

Don't just go by what you see.

EVERLASTING LIFE

The body will fade away but your spirit will never die,
The real you will have everlasting life with Christ,
Your perfect will is for us to live, despite the past
We win.
You saw our flaws.
But there's hope for a sinner,
I choose you, which is Christ,
It's good to have hope and to know the body will fade away,
But the real us will have everlasting life.
So don't worry about what man tries to do,
There's a future now, and forever for you,
It's everlasting life.
God's got something better for those who believe,
It's everlasting life.

EVERY DAY COUNTS

Look at what's happening in this world,
His peace is better,
Men are at war,
We don't know what the next day will bring,
Foundations crumble,
Man rumble,
What's going on?
Don't you know every day counts?
Why are you still playing?
Show love, everyday counts.
God sees everything.
It's always a rush life.
While you can, woman and man,
Love each other,
Everyday counts.
Enjoy the sun and peace of mind,
We can be grateful for today.
So make every day count.

EVERY NAIL WAS FOR ME

Every nail was for me,
A sinner pursuing a life of sin
He took the charge for us,
My Savior loves us,
My chains,
My sin,
An innocent man had to

take the nails on the cross for us,
This world has so many living in darkness,
Not knowing one day, we have to say
Did I live for God or for myself?
Did I become free or did I stay a slave?
A Savior had to come,
When they nailed Him to the cross, my sins were nailed too,
A man who loved us and took our sins on the cross with him,
And they nailed him to the cross,
So I can be free,
Every nail was for me.
Jesus died on the cross and rose up in 3 days with the nail prints in His hands and feet.

Joe Bull

FAITH

You won't take away my faith!

All around me there are many distractions.

Just because you want to better yourself,

Some obstacles try to get in the way.

I believe your word is true.

They want to use worry and fear to break you.

Man wants you to fear –

So they'll tell you what you can do to limit you,

That's why it takes faith.

You won't take away my faith!

You won't stop me!

I have a purpose!

I'm not lesser,

He's got more for me and you

So I'm a live by faith.

FAMILY COOKOUT

A sunny day – everyone there,

Smoke's in the air

Friends of the family and kids playing

The smell of food

People enjoying the life God gives.

Instead of worrying about your job,

Your day is about having fun,

You are grilling out – cooking for everyone.

You made this a wonderful day –

I can truly say it's a blessing

To be able to spend time with family not just during bad times,

Being at the family cookout brings us together.

Having fun and not judging anyone

And respecting everyone at the family cookout.

FIRE FOR THE COLD

Arctic air in the atmosphere,
Cold sweeping the country,
Some waking up to frost,
On the interstate they had pile ups.
May the heart of men not be cold,
You have a lot to give the world,
But it's cold out here in the homes.
We've got to love each other.
We all have flaws.
It's cold out here in these
streets.
Look around!
With this cold sweeping the nation,
Lord, may I stay close to your word?
Your word is the fire for the cold.
In this world we go through and want nothing to do with you,
And that's when we get cold.
In a cold world I have to stay close to the fire,
I don't want to be cold for You.

.

FOCUS ON WHAT MATTERS

All the evil from the dark camps

Trying to hurt hearts

With their dark plan using man.

They want us to live in fear,

And focus on something that don't even matter.

They try to put their evil in the heads of men,

God made the world,

But the evil one got man thinking he did something,

Now they want us to focus on their life and then we can't live,

Our life, so we put our hope in the Lord not this world, it'll only keep your mind on the negative.

FOR THE WHOLE WORLD TO SEE

A light that shines in the world,

A light that shines for the whole world to see,

In the libraries, coffee shops, schools, churches and more,

The light is visible for all to see, when a light shines it shows,

If it stays covered up with the layers of time, then how can it shine?

Taking the light cross the bridges of doubt and fear, letting them know there's a light in here for the whole world to see,

A light that brightens the face leaving behind smiles,

The road takes you on many journeys,

But the light that shines brightens your path.

A light that shines for the whole world to see.

FOUNDATION

All around us in the lost world,

Some don't know the hope,

Then they can't cope

Man builds and tear down,

We need a foundation in our lives that can give us peace, and that is God,

So many let you down when you've got a foundation you know,

You can depend on Him and study His word,

Jesus is the foundation for what He did for us,

Now it's up to you to believe and be set free from anxieties of this world,

Many times we let people define us, but what does God think about you?

He sent His son to die for your sins,

You have hope; a foundation that can give you peace.

GETTING PASS CLOSED DOORS

What do I do, but trust you more?

Because that door didn't open,

I won't give up, God's got something better,

I'm getting pass closed doors,

Sometimes you ask why, you didn't know what was behind the door because it was closed,

One day you will see,

What was meant for you with God in it

No one can stop,

Learn to move on and trust Him more.

I'm getting pass closed doors.

GRADUATING FROM MINDSETS

Why can't I be the unique person?

God made me!

Man wants you to focus on what limits you,

That's why the Lord is my hope,

There are mindsets that others put on you,

This year something's got to change,

Graduating from the mindsets others put on us,

That's why the word talks about renewing your mind,

This is the year of graduating from mindsets.

GRATEFUL

I'm grateful for your grace and mercy,

Where would I be if it wasn't for you,

If you know about losing, a win is a win, to be grateful for today,

If I don't have everything I want, I'm grateful I have everything I need,

I'm grateful that You allowed me to see another day,

Grateful to be able to write these poems,

Sometimes you learn to be grateful.

HATE WITH NO REASON

Hate in their faces,
They can't even smile,
But the first one to judge,
And you see the pain in the homes,
So many look to man but forget about the real provider,
How can they love if they don't know you?
Somebody disagrees with you,
then it's hate with no reason,
Do we really make it better with all this division?
I see the hate in their faces
They smile but it's not for real,
Somebody different then you, and don't have what you have but trying to make it in
What they say, "a free land?"
You just want to control it,
It becomes hate with no reason.

HE BROUGHT YOU OUT OF THE FIRE

I heard your story

I don't know how you feel,

But God is real,

He can still use you,

When you were in the fire, someone had to be there to bring you out.

Your story may have a lot of pain,

I don't know how you feel but God is real,

He sees something in you that even the fire could not burn,

You've been through the fire and didn't get burned

Maybe your story and what you been threw can help others too,

That's why he brought you out of the fire.

HE CAN USE YOU TOO

Nobody better than you,

He can use you too,

When you only put your hope in man,

You're going to be disappointed for just looking at people,

When God is the source,

He loves His children too,

Nobody better than you,

Despite past failures,

Hope has come!

Only believe you can do greater things with Him.

So if you're feeling low

This is a message for you,

Your Father in heaven loves you

Nobody better than you.

HE'S GOT MORE FOR YOU TO DO

You've experienced so much in life – the pain, and shame,

You didn't want the world to know about it,

You were here for today but living in yesterday

Now your time has come, it has come,

Fear don't own you,

You have a purpose!

There are great things for you to do,

The past couldn't defeat you,

God knows your purpose and He's got more for you to do.

HE IS UNDEFEATED

My God has never lost a fight and never will!

So why they trying to come against Him?

The plan of the enemy is to make you lose your faith,

When the pressure is on,

He wants you to be overwhelmed

When you trust God what can man do?

God is higher and bigger,

Who can stand in His way?

When man comes against you,

They're fighting against God, and don't know it,

You want to break me,

I'm a let God fight this fight,

He is undefeated.

Joe Bull

HIS PEACE IS MY FREEDOM

All around me things are going on,

Who can set us free from life's worries?

His peace is my freedom.

I can have all the other things

But what do I need in situations?

His peace is my freedom.

To hear from you I know everything will be alright,

Man wants to bring fear to keep us enslaved here,

You can't take away what you didn't give,

You might not understand me,

And think I don't care,

That only means

I know His peace is my freedom.

HIS WINNER

From your night cry, dry your eye,

We still believe in healing,

The doctor gave a bad report,

But I see you smiling, you are keeping your joy,

You know you are His winner,

No matter what the report said,

Keep your faith and trust in God,

What can separate us from Christ love?

You know you are His winner.

The world doesn't understand why you still have joy,

Nothing can separate us from Christ's love,

Whatever comes our way,

We're going to trust God

You know, man may count you out

But that don't mean you're done,

Winners start over.

I'm His winner. You're His winner.

HOPE DURING CAPTIVITY 2

Why are we the biggest prison in the world?

So many still in chains, and still in captivity.

Many have addictions and trying to be someone else, instead of who God wants them to be

What you are going through is never easy,

But do you have hope during captivity?

They give us mindsets,

But I rather have Jesus; someone who knows about being in captivity,

He's our hope so we can make it

No matter what man tries to do to us,

That's why you need the Lord to fight for you,

And to make it while in these chains,

What you're going through is never easy,

This is to give you hope during captivity,

With Jesus you are free.

HOW PRECIOUS IS TODAY

An ungrateful spirit in the atmosphere,

Some woke up this morning, and still don't know why they're here.

These days going by real fast, they're not going to always last,

How precious is today,

We have only one day at a time,

Man keeps thinking he's here forever

And keep stressing all day and want you to worry with him

What we going to do about today?

How precious is today,

If you're alive, it means something.

It's up to you!

Today is precious, Lord, what is it You want me to do?

HURT KNOWS HURT

Why are you sad?

There's a chance for you

His name is hope.

There's peace out here that the world can't give,

I know you feel bad, but live.

Christ was hurt too; he took the pain for you.

Somebody may have wronged you,

Don't let them take away your faith, no matter who it is!

You're important too!

Hurt knows hurt.

Jesus looked down and saw you,

He decided to suffer and take the hurt

Because He loves you.

I KNOW I NEED HIM

All of us have something we deal with,

We need your word, because we're not perfect,

So many worry about if they're good enough,

You need Jesus and I know I need him too,

We get tried by others, and tested just to see,

Do we really believe what we say we believe?

We stay with him and hang on in time,

We will grow and do more for Him.

I choose to stay with Jesus,

They're going to be things we go through,

Now we don't have to feel alone,

We study and fellowship with others to get stronger,

In this kind of world today we live in,

I know I need him.

I SEE HOW YOU DO THINGS

I see how you do things.

You work through ordinary people

Your angels be out here battling for us,

You be there just in time to keep us out of trouble

I see how you do things.

You protect us when we don't know we're in danger,

You deliver us from temptation,

I see how you do things.

You always have a plan,

Sometimes we don't understand,

You take the little we have and multiply it if we believe by faith.

I'M A GET THERE WITH YOU

Show me the way I can't do it alone,

This is your gift I'm using

Increase it for your glory,

So they will see your goodness,

Lord You are amazing!

You help the blind see,

I can't do it alone I need you with me,

In due season I know you will prosper whatever I do.

The future is going to be bright –

I'm a get there with you.

I'M A LET YOU LEAD THE WAY

After all the failures, it's time to go down the right roads,

The other roads lead to nowhere.

Just because He didn't show up on your time,

Doesn't mean He doesn't care, and He wasn't there,

The detours in life may take us down a longer route,

But you always have a plan for us,

We be wanting things to happen fast,

And sometimes we choose to say what you should've done,

Then say, "I'm a let you lead the way."

IN A WORLD LIKE THIS ONE

So much confusion taught by man,

Lord they trying to do it without you,

So much confusion in the world.

Starting to see the light, your word is my guide,

In a world like this we need your wisdom,

You don't want us to be confused.

You're not in confusion,

In a world like this one,

We need you more.

Who they going to look up to,

Lord we look up to you,

Why they trying to confuse a new generation,

Too much confusion out here.

This generation needs hope instead of more confusion, Lord when we put you first,

We will know how to live in a world like this one.

IN NEED OF THE SAVIOR

There's a war going on out here,

Generations are at risk, look around at the change,

More people going into chains,

 Some in higher places giving the enemy a new face,

They bring more confusion,

We don't have to have a generation of lost people,

We all have different backgrounds,

So we all have choices,

Choose good or evil.

So many hurting,

In a world in need of the Savior.

IT CAN'T STAY THE SAME

Years go by –

What can we say,

But thank the Lord for bringing us out of situations that were tough,

It can't stay the same, another level can't be living any kind of way

Be a business instead of being in someone's business,

We can't listen to those who just want the old you,

It can't stay the same.

It's up to us to do something great,

So put away the hate, stop forcing things on people,

God gives us a choice

So there's a better way

As for me, It can't stay the same.

IT MEANS SOMETHING TO HIM

It may not mean something to man,

But it means something to Him,

They want to discourage you from the blessing,

You feel like the world don't appreciate you,

But God sees you and what you do,

Keep being in His word, He will speak to you,

It may not mean something to man

But it means something to Him,

You may get overlooked by them but that's alright,

Put God first He will direct your path,

It may not mean something to man

But it means something to him.

JUST TO HEAR FROM YOU

Putting away cares at this time,

I need quiet time.

I'm looking for directions,

Man out there trying to keep us weary,

People get tired and need rest,

But on the way they get stress,

We don't learn to rest,

We been taught to build monuments and castles for someone,

But they don't talk about building your spirit up,

You get drained from the cares of the world,

I have to sit still just to hear from you.

KEEP DREAMING

I want to go to places I've never been before,

I want to see different faces

Visit other places

Owe no man,

Do a lot of giving.

You got to keep dreaming.

I want to go to places I've never been before,

See different faces and go coast to coast.

You got to keep dreaming.

I want to tell the world,

God is able and let the world know,

Peace is from above

We don't have to hurt each other

Learn to love and live in peace.

You got to keep dreaming.

KEEP MOVING AHEAD

I look at the night
and see the stars,
Who cause wars,
Who have scars from time,
But never mind,
Man's not listening to that voice that gives him a choice,
As I walk from place to place,
Wherever my feet go,
My footprints are left in time,
Who's going to heal the mind?
Can they see it or did they let the changes of time blind them?
If we keep moving ahead
We will be able to see possibilities
In time it will be yours.
Keep moving ahead.

LONELY IN THE DARK

Lonely in the dark,

You're crying on the inside,

On the outside you appear to cheer,

But closely a life of pain,

Waking up to the dark world,

Can wealth pay for love?

Inside you're still lonely,

What can replace the emptiness when you tried everything to cover up the loneliness?

There's hope in Jesus who can give you peace

So you don't have to be lonely in the dark.

LONG ROAD

The long road; it's one step at a time,

We're going to get there,

All the struggles in life all the pain in life,

But you can't win if you quit.

Only miles to go on the long road,

Lord I put my trust in you,

You are my strength to help me get there,

What can man do when you are my hope?

The road might be long,

But I'm a get there following you.

It's a long road but it's one step at a time.

LORD GUIDE ME TODAY

I see man wants to do his own things,

To try to instill fear in our minds,

How they want us to live in fear, to control us here? But our God is bigger!

Man tries to put doubt in our minds

Live one day at a time

so we can treat people right,

We're not weak in Christ, we're strong,

Live one day at a time,

The enemy want us to worry every day,

But I'm a trust the Lord today is what He gave us,

So despite what they say, I'm a go to the word,

The Lord is my strength and today is all about him,

He didn't give us a spirit of fear,

Today is what we have,

He will guide you if we wait on him,

Lord guide me today.

MIRACULOUS MEET US HERE

We're in agreement now

Miraculous meet us here.

Let the heavens open up and rain down healing,

We believe you can do it here,

You made the lame man walk and the blind see,

Miraculous meet us here.

We have to keep believing

What else is there to do?

When we put our hope in you,

Miraculous meet us here.

Meet us now.

OUR TIME AT THE BEACH

I like how you separated the water and the land
How you made the beach for man.
Freshness of the air,
I was there,
People in the waters enjoying their time
Under the sunlight at the beach.
You see people walking,
Some riding down the boulevard
That's what I saw.
They're relaxing not thinking about the cares of life.
As I walk the beach and look at the water
I thought about how some choose the beach as their fun sometimes; not everyone.
 We need you everywhere we go.
So protect us and keep us safe
Lead us away from temptation.
We came to enjoy our time at the beach in peace,
and to acknowledge you.

PEACEFUL WALK ON THE BEACH

I like looking at the water and walking on the sand,
You can tell from it looks it was from your hand.
When storms come we have to go to a place of safety,
When it leaves, we're back at the beach.
A place for the whole family to enjoy,
No need to spend your whole life worrying.
You can have fun without hurting anyone,
Or trying to keep up with someone else.
God made the beach for all of us,
We can live in peace and don't always have to be in a rush,
When the storms of life come how will we react, what do we do?
Lord we trust in you,
Sometimes a get away from the cares of the world
Is what we need,
Your getaway might be doing something else you love,
A peaceful walk on the beach is for me
It's my getaway from the cares – just for that day.

PRAY FOR TODAY'S WORLD

Prayer is needed –

Too much hate in the world.

Children are dying and men or at war with each other in the world.

Why they don't talk about the evil?

Man against man

They are taking each other out.

These mothers love their sons too.

What makes all this hate in the World,

They are making promises each year,

But trying to do it, without prayer

Every life matters, the grave is full of dead dreams,

Sounds of the dark nights screams,

While we got a chance, pray for the world.

PROTECT US DURING THE STORM

You will direct our paths and show us what to do.

There's a storm in the sea that's not so nice, they gave it a name,

For every storm; no matter what the name, it's not bigger than the name Jesus.

Peace be still.

Your word is true,

Be the shelter for those who suffer loss,

Keep the people safe

A home or other things can be replaced,

Protect us during the storm.

Now we can live in your peace and not worry.

You're bigger than any storm

Protect us during the storm.

PUSHING HIM AWAY

We need God, but keep pushing Him away.
Look around the enemy knows what he is doing,
People are hurting themselves and others.
They don't know who they are,
We're a free country but we still have to have respect for each other.
We need God, but keep pushing Him away.
We're losing babies,
It is getting more and more crazy out here,
They don't want God in their business,
But He blesses businesses.
What do you need from God?
He made the world,
But some thinks He's after their fun
So they push him away.
We have to have respect for each other,
The next generation don't have to fade,
This world needs God,
But keep pushing Him away.

REDEMPTION

Who's going to be the one to encourage you during your trials?

Will you talk about me or support me?

When I'm at my lowest,

I know someone who won't just talk about you,

He is there for you,

And His words are healing,

You didn't count me out,

Man remembered the bad,

But you say I'm forgiven,

We all fall short that's why we run to you,

We don't have to stay down,

Now I can move on,

Even though we had a past,

Now we have a future in you,

That's redemption.

Joe Bull

RUNNING THE RACE

The race is on,

So many dropping out,

Life's road was too rough on their feet,

They didn't see a finish line,

In life you keep living,

It's not over 'til it's over,

You still living,

And this is not the last trophy you will see,

Stay in the race, many challenges we will face,

God is the one watching you run,

You're looking back to much,

While getting passed,

Others want to win,

Then when we open our eyes,

There's no   line,

You're still alive, In the end,

He's going to see how you ran your race,

God gave us the breath for the race,

Which is your life and legacy,

Will you keep the faith and finish the race?

You're still alive, there's time to get to know His word and get understanding,

The Father in heaven wants to talk to you,

While you are running the race.

SEE MY HEART

See my heart,

I can look up and don't let my ways keep me away from you.

I have not reached perfection,

But I listen to your voice.

I have a ways to go but I believe some things are here to test us, so you can bless us.

Some say I'm a pray for you,

In time your prayers will be answered.

Your strength is perfect in my weakness.

See my heart

So I'm a move on

Man can't judge me.

They look at every move I make to see if I'm a make a mistake,

But you're the judge that sees my heart.

SHAKE THE DUST OFF

They may have rejected you or let you go but it's not over,

Sometimes you're going to feel some type of way,

The Lord understands,

Shake the dust off!

you got places to go and people to meet,

Shake the dust off

There's more opportunities,

You going to be a blessing elsewhere,

So many don't know what to do,

It takes faith to keep moving as long as we keep moving, so don't quit!

We win.

Shake the dust off and keep moving.

SHE ONE THAT SHINES

She the one that shines,

And the others see her light,

You were made for this moment.

The crowd stood up on their feet,

To witness an amazing sight,

Here comes the bride,

Coming down the aisle in all white,

As the crowd witness an amazing sight,

You shine, they see your light.

So as time passes, this love will be tested like all relationships,

But it takes trusting in God,

To keep making it.

She the one that shines,

And the others see her light.

SIN'S SLAVERY

They keep carrying them away in chains,
Because nobody talks about it,
How something starts,
With the temptation everywhere,
You do have a choice,
But sometimes people make wrong choices.
Sin wants to own you.
How can you win if your life is dominated by sin?
A prisoner in his own sin,
God can break the chains away.
How can you win if your life is dominated by sin?
We thankful for grace,
I know someone who will give you another chance
Others may talk about you but our Savior loves you
and will forgive you,
Sin's slavery ends today!
Jesus has the key if you want to be free
You no longer have to be sin's slave.

SOME DAYS WILL BE RAINY

Reflections of the trials and all the tests,
You brought me out of rainy days into sunny ones,
I hope I didn't take the sunny days for granted,
It was a chance to enjoy the sunshine,
In life, some days will be rainy, but the Lord will provide,
I know a place that has shelter during the rain,
I don't put all my trust in man,
He will put you out in the rain,
When it rains it's not always bad,
It's a chance to be inside with your family.
Some days will be rainy,
And we hear the sound of rain that falls from above,
While you have a chance, enjoy the sunshine
and appreciate it,
Because some days will be rainy.

SUNSHINE AFTER THE STORM

Despite what anyone said,

You got to believe for yourself.

It's a brand-new day

 You made it through the storm

 All the doubts and obstacles that was in your way you left them behind,

You made it with God's help

Anything's possible

Now you see the sunshine after the storm.

Dreamers know a better day is coming.

We can look up and see the sunshine after the storm.

We thank God for his safety and allowing us to see the sunshine after the storm.

TELL THEM IT'S NOT OVER

This is for the one that may not have the words to say,

After they let you go or someone gave up on you,

Or you been losing for years and tired of it,

Remember how the Lord brought His people out of bondage,

When the world tells you that you are done,

Tell them it's not over,

When you put your trust in the Lord,

You move on to do great things,

Tell them it's not over.

THAT STILL SMALL VOICE

It's the one you never hear about.

He was there before the bright lights,

The one who tells you,

Everything's going to be alright,

A true friend that encourages you,

You remember the *Voice* from above,

That tells you not to fear.

That *Still Small Voice* tells me,

To keep going forward and not to worry,

He is there for me.

I hear that *Still Small Voice*.

Joe Bull

THE KINGDOM WILL NEVER CLOSE DOWN

There was a small town far from here,
They love Friday nights and Sunday mornings,
On Friday they would watch their high school games,
Sunday morning they will be in church,
They had a plant that was most of the town's livelihood, then one day the plant closed.
Some didn't know what to do,
But you was letting them know in your word,
To trust in you, that means by faith,
There's something better.
We don't just sit around and worry,
They took away what was never ours,
The plant is an empty building now,
And it's time to move on
so what do you have left?
People leave and places close down on you,
But His word will stand,
The Kingdom will never close down.

THE MORNING SUNRISES OVER THE WATERS

Lord I appreciate all your art rising over the waters,
Before my eyes a spectacular sight,
It's so amazing to see such a beautiful sight!
It's before my eyes.
It's amazing how He does it.
Only God can command the sun to rise,
What a sight for all nations to gather around to see.
Sometimes we don't realize the beauty that's before our eyes, like the morning sunrise.
Lord there's nothing you can't do,
You woke me up early that morning to see the morning sun coming up over the waters,
The Morning Sunrise over the waters.

THE WINGS THAT BELONG TO YOU

She felt bad when it wasn't going her way.
They didn't tell her God is the way,
Only believe He will give you more strength to live
Your life with joy and more peace,
You was meant to soar with the wings that belong to you.
You can fly above any obstacles distractions and sickness that be in the way,
You may be in a season and feel like you are being kept down,
But with these wings you're able to soar, you're able to fly.
Sometimes you feel like you're not going higher but your situation won't stop your purpose,
These are the wings that belong to you that they can never take,
You were meant to fly,
the wings that belong to you
With God's help,
you can live and soar above any obstacle, distraction, and sickness that be in the way,
The wings that belong to you.

THERE'S A LOT TO LIVE FOR

That's the plan of the enemy for you to destroy yourself,
Then he will go find someone else
Do you feel like it's the end?
Please give life another look,
There's a lot to live for,
You're special to him
Don't worry about them.
It's Ok, Jesus know your pain,
They put nails through His body,
He loves you so much
He stayed on the cross, died and rose,
Just for you and others.
If you think it's the end, look again
There's someone to talk to,
Somebody that loves you.
Whatever it is, give it to him,
Be free – the past is over.
There's a lot to live for,
God's got a future for you.

THERE'S HOPE FOR YOU TOO

The world threw you away,

Because you use to live any kind of way,

But God didn't throw you away,

Only believe,

Take one day at a time,

You are not the only one who had a past,

Even you can be saved,

God forgives,

Are you ready to move ahead?

The past is behind you.

He believes in you – Jesus loves you.

There's hope for you too.

TILL I GET THERE

Till I get there He's still working on me and you,

But there still a chance to learn to fly like the eagle,

My problems I give to Him,

Till I get there,

I have to keep studying His word,

He strengthens me more in time

Over all my weaknesses,

Till I get there, I'm a keep learning and being patient,

It's a journey, you not alone,

As long as you have faith, there's hope,

Till you get there.

WATER IN A DRY PLACE

In the desert searching for water,

A dry place in need of water,

Desperate for it,

I had to get away from the cares,

In need of the miraculous,

A place where it is dry,

But you can make water come up out of the ground, In a place they said was no hope,

You still the same God,

After we put away these other gods and then we can watch the true God cause water to spring up in that dry place.

WELCOME

Here comes the One who welcomes you with open arms,

It's not easy, we heard your story,

But did they tell you about the Savior who wants you to give your burdens to Him?

He doesn't want you worrying,

Jesus knows what you've been through,

That's why He is a true friend that loves you,

He wants to welcome you,

The Lord will continue to work on you,

We probably don't know all you've been through,

But He knows, and wants to welcome you.

All His angels will celebrate over you.

WHAT ARE YOU DOING HERE

Sometimes in life, fear tries to keep us from moving.

Fear makes us feel like we're alone.

We don't want to go anywhere,

Then we get weak,

But we have to hear God speak,

He didn't tell you to stay there.

What are you doing here?

He chose you for His purpose.

Fear tries to keep you from moving,

Rise up and eat!

You're going to need your strength.

Who told you to stay in fear?

What are you doing here?

He chose you for His purpose.

WHAT DO YOU SEE

Tell me what do you see?

Your vision got blurry from the cares of the world,

Too much of everything else, but not enough of God.

He said write the vision down and make it plain,

They say you plan to fail if you don't plan,

But if God gave you a vision then He can also give you the plan,

Sometimes we have to be still and hear Him instead of looking at the circumstances,

That's why we see people as trees,

In need of another touch,

Sometimes our vision gets blurry

That's why we need Him more.

WHAT TO DO ABOUT THE FLESH

It was that moment of living,

Just in it for that moment,

But there's a price to pay for not listening,

Pleasure like that just don't last,

Pain comes after that,

In an appointed time, you leave out walking on fire,

Not knowing everything is about to expire,

If it was just all in your mind,

Then you tell the flesh to shut up,

But you may be caught in drama

And don't know what to do,

You keep going back to that place,

You don't know what to do,

Open His word and read it

From now on,

Let God lead you.

WHEN DO WE MAKE TIME FOR YOU?

I don't want the cares of the world to take away my quiet time with you,

In these times there are so many distractions,

Sometimes we forget about what's important,

Not everyone can see the little things are being taken away,

But God is still the same,

We can't let the relationship get cold,

So many other things to do,

When do we make time for you?

WHEN EVERYONE IS LOOKING FOR YOU

Lord this world needs You more,

When everyone is looking for you, it will be a better place.

In this lost world so many don't know who they are, they're listening to the ones who only want a position,

They can't find you because they're looking elsewhere,

When everyone is looking for you, there'll be revivals not just shows,

You are still the same God; a miraculous God that saves souls.

When everyone is looking for you, people will be set free.

WHO'S IN CHARGE OF THE SHIP

He knows it hurts but the past is gone

You're still acting out what happened to you years ago,

We're supposed to let Jesus be the captain,

Why we still trying to stir the ship?

We keep running into waves, we're supposed to let Jesus be the captain,

We keep going in the wrong directions,

If you're free from your past and Jesus is the captain

Then you will move ahead instead of backwards,

He knows you been hurt – it's not easy,

We don't know how you feel but He knows,

So who's in charge of the ship?

Are you going to keep going places you don't need to go or let Jesus take charge on the ship?

WHY WOULD YOU WANT TO GO BACKWARDS

So many say they miss the old days
You say it in your talk,
What you know or don't know today is a blessing
the past was a lesson.
God brought you from poverty's mindsets to be
blessed and highly favored
He healed you many times,
If we believe His words and don't doubt,
We don't have to keep looking back
Now we can look ahead because we
win,
Finally you've learned to do things better and trust
in Christ
He blessed you so much and brought you out of so
much,
Why would you want to go backwards.

WRITING TO THE HURTING

Nobody knows what you're going through,

You try to move forward but you're letting the past define who you are now,

This is my prayer for you,

That you let the One who made you take charge,

You're hurting but God has never lost a fight,

Your outward may be hurt but your spirit inside, the enemy will not touch,

I'm writing this to the hurting,

Jesus wants to comfort you,

we don't know what you're going through,

He wants to give you a future and hope,

Take it one day at a time, have faith, all things are possible.

YOU CAN BE ON HIS TEAM

They didn't pick you and now you disappointed because they didn't call your name
When the crowd wouldn't let you ride with them, you felt shame
Let me tell you about a team that ranks # 1 and is not done
We're still winners even when we fail,
He never counts us out
I know you feel left out
but you are a winner
you can be on His team
His team wins the championship every year.
On this team, we don't worry about what you look like on the outside or how many people knows you,
God knows you and we walk by faith not by sight.
Don't worry about them when you can be on His team.

YOU'RE GOING PLACES

You was hanging around that mountain for a while,

You been giving a brand-new day and a bigger smile

You're going places.

It's not too late,

You don't have to be comfortable,

God's got so many places you've never been before,

You're going places.

It's not too late

You are about to do great things in different places,

Only believe

God's got so much for you to see,

You're going places.

YOUR ANGELS

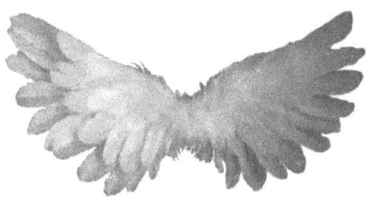

You hide me in your wings

When they thought they had me,

That's when you protected me from the enemies I can't see

All around us a lot is going on

There's no need to fear, your angels are here.

Now I can rest

There more of them than us,

Your angels are all around us.

YOUR HOPE KEEPS ME

Lord, all around me I need your help,

I keep wanting to do more and go more places,

I'm in the same place but I can't let my feelings

Make me act out of impatience

because I want something more

I have to use faith and move on,

Soon You will show me why I had to stay in a place,

Where I'm ready to leave and still there,

It won't be long now,

Soon you will reveal more to me

It's not too late

We ask ourselves why am I still in a place I want out of,

Having faith is what going to get you out,

God knows your heart,

We don't have all the answers,

But He gives us hope that better is coming,

I'm grateful that your hope is what's keep me going.

A TALK WITH YOU CHANGES EVERYTHING

She was struggling for many years...

How long will she keep going to the well?

You may have given up and think it's done

But let me tell you about someone

His love for you is no ordinary love,

Where people keep leaving you,

This love is the truth.

Despite your past, there's someone you can talk to.

You may feel like you have to be like someone else, but couldn't find it at the well.

I don't know what is your well,

If you can't find peace, a talk with Jesus changes everything.

A PLACE TO TRAIN WITH NO DISTRACTIONS

Sometimes we have to go to a place to train with no distractions,

What happened to the hunger and thirst for His word,

You used to pray more and be in His word,

Then you let the cares of the world takeover,

Sometimes we have to go to a place to train with no distractions and leave with revelation and a strong spirit,

What happened to that fire in your eyes,

You started letting the storms of life take your attention off of him,

You might have to get up early but don't listen to the ones that are satisfied

They're comfortable,

It starts now!

Sometimes we must go to a place to train with no distractions.

NEW GENERATION

Don't worry about fitting in,

There's a lot to live for,

You're going to have so call friends or life friends.

People who speak positive things to you, are for you

This is for the young people who might have gone the wrong way

I know a real friend that forgives and His name is Jesus

So-called friends don't know what fun is,

You don't talk down on other people.

God will give you wisdom young people,

Learn to listen.

He has a lot for you to do

Some think it's about fitting in,

A new Generation, God made you for a purpose.

A NAME THAT'S POWERFUL

Who can stand against you?

The armies of darkness is trying to take your family down with them,

But we speak Jesus to them, they won't prevail

We send them back to the pits of hell.

Jesus name is so powerful we break the hands of poverty and lack

And He defends us from those who want to just take,

You give us the power to get wealth,

We speak Jesus over our finances and our family,

No army from hell can stop what you've got for us.

A FATHER TO TALK TO

They need a father to talk to... Is this why you do what you do, just for a father to talk to you?
We all have flaws and need someone to talk to,
Society is teaching, but too many fathers they are not reaching,
You're not always going to have fancy things or be like someone you see in a video,
Do we care that fathers are dying in the streets and getting locked away because sometimes society thinks they're weak when they love people and do what's right,
But these same people think it's cool to be in man's chains,
All we hear are sirens going down the road,
So much hate out here because we are all different and don't agree,
Lord we look to you to give us wisdom, we can talk to you
Father's day can be every day if we put YOU first,
We are never alone because we can talk to you.

A CRY OUT HERE

One minute they're here, then they're gone,
Now you say I'm alone,
There's a cry out here in homes and in the streets,
Watch these generations closely,
All the hurt out here, all the hate our here,
There's a cry out here in homes and in the streets,
It's time for some good news, where so many hurting each other; the time is now.
There's a cry out here,
Who's going to tell them the truth,
The future is at stake,
Watch these generations closely,
Put God first.
These distractions out here, wants to get your attention,
While people are going into chains,
There's a cry out here in homes and in the streets.

THE OTHER GIANTS

It was good to hear about how David defeated Goliath,

But what about the other giants we face which took his place,

Whether it's the giant of distraction or intimidation and other things, the battle is the Lord's,

They want to have us living in fear,

That's the plan,

But for now I'm going to put it all in God's hand,

What they don't realize, He sees everything and reads every heart,

They think they are winning but the wicked wealth is stored up for the just,

Sometimes the giant can be us,

They don't talk about the other giants,

Man thinks he has won, but you're going to always need help down the road,

When the next giant show you, There's going to be some help from above,

You won't be able to do it alone against the other giants,

You're going to need some help,

Be strong in the Lord and allow God to defeat the other giants.

RELATIONSHIP

Where do I be when you're ready to talk?

Do I let distractions keep me from hearing your voice?

I still want to walk with you and really share my thoughts with you

Sometimes I hear everything else but your voice,

I have to get back in relationship with You,

Relationships supposed to grow.

What do you say when the relationship is from a distance?

Prayer still works if you're far away,

You can get back in the relationship,

Before you give up, think again.

After the trials, will you be with your true friend

This is a relationship,

We don't always do right and have all the answers,

but I can still talk to someone who won't judge but give me hope.

Sorry for the days I ignore you Lord,

That's why it's a relationship – we have to keep talking.

A WINNING ATMOSPHERE

You will have peace in him; it's a Winning atmosphere.

All those losses, it's time to win! Put no trust in man but in Him.

This is a new time to celebrate. You are about to do Great Things.

You will have peace in Him, this a Winning Atmosphere.

Even when things or some giants stand in the way, the battle is His I can keep my peace,

Remember this is when the Giants show up again. This is your fight every day.

You will have peace in Him, this a Winning Atmosphere.

He knows what you are going through.

His peace is what makes it, a winning atmosphere.

You will have peace in Him – This a Winning Atmosphere.

A BETTER WAY

There are a lot hurting people out here,

We may not always understand them,

Everyday someone gets carried away,

We can't stop everything

What we can say there's a better way,

So much positive we can do instead fighting ourselves and hurting people,

There's a better way when we put God first

Not that we're perfect but know who is our source.

There's a better way, I put my trust in You,

I don't have to worry about what man tries to do,

The battle is the Lord's, no more time to waste

There's a better way.

WATERFALL POURING DOWN BLESSINGS

What you've been going through nobody knew,

You were at that place where the water falls,

Every day you need a word that will help you,

This is not the end,

As the waters pour this moment you'll never forget

God keeps pouring down blessings

All you hear is the sound of water.

Peace and love is in the atmosphere

You don't think about the cares of the world here.

Old mindsets are washed away.

Waters pouring down

That's what makes the waterfall so great.

THE WAVES KEEP MOVING

Not just waves in the sea when we look upon You're in the sunlight.

You are forever moving as the water is pushed, the waves keep moving.

There's no comparison

Each wave is unique,

As I stand on the sand under the sunlight

I see a wave that gets my attention,

But after a while there's a new wave,

They keep moving.

I can watch waves at the beach all day,

But like them I've got to keep moving.

PUTTING THE PAST BEHIND YOU

Society have its picks,

Trying to make you feel you didn't make their team,

But look to the ONE who sent His Son for those who believe,

My past I give to Him,

Forgive me for my sins,

He has a place for the ones who society overlooks.

You made it!

The past is over,

It's time to move forward,

I'm putting the past behind me.

NEVER SMALL

Don't let nobody tell you what you can do.

No matter where you come from or who you know.

You're somebody special in his eyes.

Hey it's ok

We all have a past but in His eyes you're never small

We speak things over ourselves, but God didn't say we were small.

He's got great things for you to do

You're never small

That's the way He sees you.

FAITH OVER NUMBERS

You were meant to be here

that's why He chose you,

I come in the name of the Lord,

I have faith over numbers

To the world, it looks like you can't win

And they say the odds are against you,

None of it is true

Lord I'm a trust in you, that's what makes me

VICTORIOUS

When there's not a lot of people to have your back,

We get caught up in the numbers,

It's meant to be to test me to see how I would react

If only one showed up will I choose faith over numbers?

They say loser... He says **WINNER!**

What do you say?

we get too caught up in the numbers,

I come in the name of the Lord,

To the world it looks like you can't win,

While they say the odds are against you,

None of it is true,

You might be the one He chooses to do great things for Him.

The next time it looks like you're not winning,

Choose faith over numbers.

SURVIVAL SKILLS

We've been taught that only certain ones can have blessings,

In a world where you learn to survive,

They don't talk about how to live

When you see people around, you're teaching survival skills.

They say Jesus is the way and never talk about the abundant life He has for us.

But in time, I had to unlearn some things

That taught me only survival

When God have an abundant life for us.

EITHER WAY I'M A WINNER

Now they say the odds are against you, but that what man say,

My hope is in the lord no matter what man try to do,

You never said the odds was against me that's what man said,

If you take away something from me, that means He allow me to move on,

He has better, either way I'm a winner because I acknowledged him as my Savior, and trust him

He has better.

BE FREE

I see the chains broken, no more stuck in mindsets,
Freedom is not free when you're chained to man's ideology,
Who wants to be in bondage?
When you trust God, He will give you a chance to be free,
No more poverty
Yes God can break any chain,
To be free from these mindsets, we have to study His Word,
In due time, if I stay focused on you, I'll walk on my situation,
Every problem I give to you.
Live to be free!

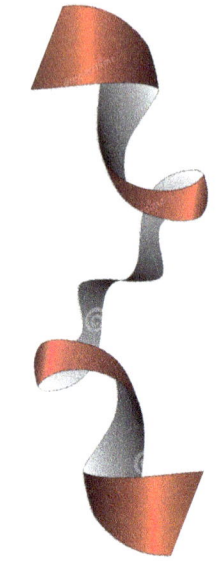

I HAVEN'T HEARD FROM YOU IN AWHILE

There's a knock at the door.

Who did I see?

That lost son,

Who I haven't heard from in a while,

He had a big smile,

I remember we used to talk more

Until he went far away

And did it his way,

I'm glad to see him again,

He came home and told me his story,

All the blessings and gifts his father gave him,

He thought the world would love him,

But when everything was spent up,

They told him he had to go,

He was betrayed,

He forgot about his father's love,

He realized, "I know somebody who really loves me!"

Then I told him, It's still good to see you,

I haven't heard from you in a while,

It's good to see you son.

YOUR PURPOSE IS NOT DEAD.

Call forth your purpose; it's not dead it just a sleep.

Don't let them make you feel it's over,

Just because of your age and your past.

You tried many things, except doing your purpose,

You can call forth that dream you've wanted to do,

It may have been wrapped in grave clothes,

But your purpose was not dead.

We allowed it to sleep.

God's got great things for you to do

Your purpose is not dead.

WALKING THROUGH THE FIRE

Out of the fire, man may put obstacles in the way,

He wants to discourage you,

But I believe your angel is around to protect you while you are in the fire,

When God's glory be on us,

The fire has no power,

So they may try to bring fear,

Some may feel it's over for you,

But can't see you are walking through the fire.

HEALING IS IN THIS PLACE

Healing is in this place!

By faith and agreement we believe in healing

No matter what someone said,

You're going to be healthy and won't have to stay in a bed,

Healing is in this place now.

By faith and agreement you believe His word is true,

Healing is in this place!

Only believe.

The power of God is in the atmosphere,

Healing is here and healing is in this place.

He looks at your faith.

With God nothing is impossible.

YOU ARE ABOUT TO DO GREAT THINGS TOO

He never saw you as too small,

You've been told by man what you can do,

But God has great things for you to do,

You may have given up because of an experience,

This is the time to step out on faith

Forget what they told you,

Past success was good but this is a new day,

I have a word for you, it encouraged me and I hope these poems have encouraged you!

You are about to do Great Things too.

Poems inspired by reading the Bible and life experiences.

ABOUT THE AUTHOR

Joseph Bull - 1971 is a South Carolina resident. He  was born in Darlington where he attended public schools. He is a graduate of Mayo High School.

Joe, as he is affectionately called by his family and peers, has always had a love for the arts. He sees poetry in the same light. His poetry is the art of words. His skill for writing spans 20 years or more. This prophetic poet gives life changing metaphor that are tastefully transforming.

Joe has an incredible work ethic which he has honed since he was a very young fellow. Joe held many retail dept management positions and is consistent to this day. Even with a rigorous schedule, he finds time for his family, his local assembly, Abundant Life Church, and writing. He wrote his first book in 2019 entitled You Are About To Do Great Things. Mr. Bull is married and resides in the Pee Dee area. He continues to write poetry for the sheer joy of it and inspiration to others.